Stoicism

A Deeper Insight Into Stoic Principles and Practices

Garry Hudson

The contents of this book may not be reproduced, duplicated or transmitted without direct written permission from the author.

Under no circumstances will any legal responsibility or blame be held against the publisher for any reparation, damages, or monetary loss due to the information herein, either directly or indirectly.

Legal Notice:

This book is copyright protected. This is only for personal use. You cannot amend, distribute, sell, use, quote or paraphrase any part or the content within this book without the consent of the author.

Disclaimer Notice:

Please note the information contained within this document is for educational and entertainment purposes only. Every attempt has been made to provide accurate, up to date and reliable complete information. No warranties of any kind are expressed or implied. Readers acknowledge that the author is not engaging in the rendering of legal, financial, medical or professional advice. The content of this book has been derived from various sources. Please consult a licensed professional before attempting any techniques outlined in this book.

By reading this document, the reader agrees that under no circumstances are is the author responsible for any losses, direct or indirect, which are incurred as a result of the use of information contained within this document, including, but not limited to, —errors, omissions, or inaccuracies.

© Copyright 2018 Dibbly Publishing.

All rights reserved.

Contents

CONTENTS 5

INTRODUCTION..1

CHAPTER 1 THE APPEARANCE OF A STOIC 7
    OUTWARD APPEARANCE..8
    IDENTIFYING A STOIC..10

CHAPTER 2 PERCEPTION OF A STOIC 13
    REFLECTION..20
    REAL-TIME EFFECTS OF REFLECTION..................................23
    PERCEPTION 28

CHAPTER 3 THE CHARACTER OF A STOIC 31
    THE MORALS OF LONGEVITY 35

CHAPTER 4 MINIMALISM OF A STOIC 41
    SEPARATING THE BODY FROM THE MIND.............................45
    MINIMALISM AND FASTING 48
    CURBING THE PRIMAL MIND 52

CHAPTER 5 THE DISCIPLINE OF A STOIC 61
    HABITS 62
    CHANGING TRAJECTORY 66
    NO RIGHT OR WRONG 68
    BEING IN STATE...70

CHAPTER 6 MEDITATIONS OF A STOIC..........................75
    COMPARING THE STATES OF CONSCIOUSNESS 76
    MEDITATION 79

CONCLUSION 83

Dibbly Publishing

Dibbly Publishing publishes books that inspire, motivate, and teach readers. Through lessons and knowledge.

Our Book Catalog

Visit https://dibblypublishing.com for our full catalog, new releases, and promotions.

Follow Us on Social Media

Facebook - @dibblypublishing

Twitter - @DibblyPublish

Wait! Before You Continue Reading, Download Your FREE 1000+ Affirmations eBook!

Includes Readers Newsletter

Sign up to our newsletter to receive news on new book releases, discounts, and free Kindle book promotions. All books will be available as paperback, audio, on Kindle and Kindle Unlimited unless otherwise stated. We focus on publishing books that can help people in all aspects of life on a variety of topics. Start your learning journey today!

http://dibblypublishing.com/free-affirmations-ebook

Introduction

We tend to regard Stoicism as a religion or teaching that lays out a set of rules for us to follow and then hope to be able to live a life that is peaceful and fulfilling. It doesn't work that way. Stoicism confers peace of mind and soul to the true practitioner but a true practitioner is not the product of rules, laws, and edicts. A true practitioner is one who is able to silence the chaos and observe the nature of life.

Stoicism is about the natural order and singularity of things. Stoicism is not opposed to technology, it sees it as an extension of knowledge. Stoicism does not see shapes, sizes, and color; it sees intention. Stoicism does not see right and wrong, good or bad; it sees things for what they are. Stoicism is not binary. It is all encompassing.

This book goes beyond the teachings a beginner looks for to understand the superficial elements of the Stoic virtue. This book goes beyond mere quotations and relics, icons and appearances. This book dives into the nature of life—all of life, and our place in it and how life forms us as we affect all things around us. To be Stoic is not to be sedate. To be Stoic is about knowing that there is something more and that "something more" is not concerned with mere simplistic classifications of virtue and vice. It is concerned with the ultimate understanding of the nature of life and the universe that life is a part of.

As you make your way throughout this book, you will begin to get an insight into the foundation of a Stoic's nature. You will also start to understand the reason Stoics do things the way they do. Stoicism is the art of being one with nature—and by nature I certainly do not mean the birds and the trees. By referring to nature, I am talking about the spirit of creation.

Everything that you come into contact with in this universe is made from the same building blocks as you are, and the Stoic sees this clearly. Try to look around you and find the common element between you and your dog, cat, or whatever pet you have. Try to see what is common with you and the chair you are sitting on. Try to find what is common with you and the land that you stand on. Look around you as you try to find what differentiates you from your surroundings. Take your time in doing this because the first obvious response to these questions is not usually the right one. These are the building blocks of what a Stoic is made of.

A Stoic is very aware of the wood from which he is carved and the air that is around him and within him. A Zen monk once wrote that when the wave realizes that it is just water, it has reached its enlightenment. In those terms you can look at a Stoic as the person who is one small step short of that enlightenment. Saying that a Stoic is not fully enlightened bears no intention to insult or trivialize the power of the Stoic. Rather, it is in keeping with his wishes to avoid such labels of grandeur. Humility, and the insistence that there is so much more to know than he already does, is the virtue of a Stoic. His constant pursuit of knowledge, going deeper at every turn, separates his understanding of the universe at a fundamental level. He doesn't just see the sun rise and set on a daily basis; he uses his mind to understand the occurrence deeply and intimately, while he silences all else that distracts him from coming to the realization of what everything is.

As an exercise, you should stop for a moment and think about some of the things that you don't know. When my kids were around seven to 10, I gave them an exercise to do on a daily basis. I would have each prepare a sheet of paper and write down the things they didn't know when they read a book. That did two things. First, it kept them on the lookout for anything they didn't know—words, concepts, phrases, facts, and all manner of things. As long as they had no idea what it was, I would tell them to write it down.

Once they were done, I would make them put it in an old shoebox labeled "Known Unknowns." If what they were reading was schoolwork then they would need to research what was an unknown. But if it wasn't schoolwork then they would just write it down and place it in the shoebox. When they had free time, they would just go into the box, pick up a page, and pick an item that they had placed on that sheet.

Once they did that, they would then write down what they researched and what they found out and then write down on a piece of paper the thing that they converted to knowledge and place it in another shoebox labeled "Known Knowns."

So now they had two boxes with sheets of paper filling them up. As you can imagine, the boxes filled up disproportionately, The Known Unknowns filled up fast, while the Known Knowns were slow to build.

Then there was a third box, and I told them to label it as "Unknown Unknowns." This concept lit a fire in their eyes because it was something that their little minds could not quite make out. To most adults that box would be perplexing as well. But I told them to label it anyway, without much explanation, and after a few weeks of doing this, we pulled out the three boxes and sat down together, going over the stuff that was in the Known Knowns and then in the Known Unknowns.

As you might expect, the Known Knowns box was populated but limited. It was nowhere the volume that the Known Unknowns were at, as you can imagine. Then we came to the Unknown Unknowns and the box was, as you would expect, empty. So we talked about it and I related to the kids that the three boxes come into sequence. The journey starts with Unknown Unknowns, then goes to Known Unknowns, and then finally comes to Known Knowns. The last box shows us how much we know. The middle box shows us how much we don't know. But the first box is what defines the difference between wisdom and nothingness. For the man who thinks that the empty box means nothing, his life is doomed. Not because of how little he knows, but for thinking that if he doesn't know it, it doesn't exist.

A Stoic looks at life and ponders the things that are in that first box. He can't just find them in books, but he can find them in nature and the world around him if he just opens his mind's eye and observes how everything interacts with everything else. When he makes this a habit, a light turns on within him and his senses wake up to the things that he has to do to fill up that first box. And at that point, that man becomes like the wave that realizes it is water.

Chapter 1

The Appearance of a Stoic

This book retraces the steps of a Stoic. It starts with the way he appears—silent and strong—and carves its way across the rhymes and reasons of his nature. Each scratch reveals what's beneath the skin, until we pass his flesh and bones and discover the soul of a Stoic.

The outward appearance of a Stoic is unmistakable. They appear calm, sober, and while their lips are generally silent, their eyes are never vacant. The verb *stoic* has also become an adjective in literary lexicons that shows the temperament of a person's behavior, especially under pressure.

Appearance is a good place to start when we investigate the nature of the Stoic mindset, because the outward act is always a good place to instill and propagate inward grace. It is the same reason why we go for a walk to feel better or conduct a ritual to change our fortunes. All these acts in the physical world have a measurable and distinct impact on the way we feel inside. That then turns around and influences the way we respond, the way we think, the things we believe, and so on. So the outward appearance is a good place to start.

However, I must note that stopping here would be unwise. Only looking at the outward appearance runs the risk of making your efforts superficial and fake.

The appearance of the Stoic is a reflection of the waters beneath. There is no way that you will find a body of water that is tumultuous beneath and calm above. What is underneath will be reflected at the surface and this is apparent and central to the Stoic.

At the heart of this book is the notion that those reading it are looking to understand Stoicism from afar and/or to consider whether they have it in them to embrace it. A natural Stoic is a person who instinctively, like Marcus Aurelius, recognizes his own cogitations and powers. That power is something that all of us have if we follow a specific path. And if you read intently, you will find what you are looking for in this book.

Outward Appearance

How you dress, the shoes you prefer, the colors you choose, and even the hair you keep are all outward appearances of an inner state of being. That inner state may be one that has already defined how a person wants the world to see him, at least in his mind. But nonetheless, that notion defines the way he appears. The Stoic doesn't expect anything from the world around him but is willing to contribute all he can. His lack of expectations of others leads the Stoic to disregard what others think of him because their standards where it matters, in truth and peace, are more than what most others can even come close to. Even though he is willing to give them a chance to give their opinions, those opinions fall short of any sway that they can have on his own perspective of himself. Because of this, the outward appearance of a Stoic is one that is crafter form within himself and not from the fleeting fashion of the outside world.

That is not to say that the Stoic is dressed shabbily or without a sense of decorum. The appearance of a Stoic is one of sophistication without flare, taste without pomp, and refinement without exaggeration. The Stoic doesn't spend copious amount of resources on outward appearances because he knows the true value of the external projection. His style is his own and he dresses for an audience of one—himself.

If you are on your path to understanding Stoicism, then the first thing that you should start with is the outward appearance of a Stoic and train yourself to decipher the outfit and the poise. Men typically dress to exude confidence. The less confident they truly are, the more they make up for it in their appearance. This does two things. First, it covers up the momentary deficit, and second, it is a known psychological fact that an outward act will result in an inward grace. So if you dress confidently, you will feel confident—not the other way around. A really confident man could walk naked, if it was legally accepted.

A Stoic feels confident without the need to do two things that are commonly mistaken. He doesn't need to project his confidence to tell others around him that he is confident, and second, he doesn't need symbols to light the fire of confidence within him. He is naturally confident due to his connection with the rest of the universe.

As such, a Stoic's outward appearance is one of simplicity—to the extent of being decent according to the norms of his surroundings. His appearance is also one that does not serve the purpose of making him feel grander or larger than he already is. A Stoic may wear a million-dollar watch, but it is not to make himself feel good about it. A Stoic may wear a million-dollar shoe, but it is not to brandish the designer's mark. He may wear these things because the Stoic is typically characterized by the refined nature that parallels the mind of someone who understands.

Identifying a Stoic

A Stoic can easily be picked out of a crowd if you know what to look for. It is not a necessary condition that he be expensively dressed, nor is it a certainty that his appearance will be meticulously crafted. The Stoic doesn't take excessive time to do these things, but he takes enough time to display his refinement. The former Prime Minister of Singapore, Mr. Lee Kwan Yew, was as Stoic as they get. He built a country from its early days of independence to the point of it rising up in the world today to be labeled a First World country. Even though his wealth was eventually large, and his power was pervasive across all matters in the island nation, he would wear spotlessly clean and meticulously stitched suits that were 15- to 30-years old. And he would rotate those suits, but you would never know it. He didn't splash out for stylish suits, but he was always meticulously put together. Upon close inspection, you could detect the age of the suit, but not a single thread would be out of place.

Marcus Aurelius was similar in this way. He dressed the part of the emperor, but his trappings never altered or influenced the demons in him. He knew exactly what he was made of and exactly how he was to appear, and none of that raised or inflated his inward confidence.

Back to identifying a Stoic.

If you find a person that is refined yet unbothered by his clothes then you will probably find a Stoic standing in his shoes. A Stoic never says that he is a Stoic, so walking up to him and saying, "Are you a Stoic?" will not get you the answer that you are looking for. A Stoic is not a status or a membership and a person who is Stoic doesn't necessarily know that he is. Especially today, when there is a resurrection on the virtues of the Stoic philosophy and the added attention given to the man that fits the definition, a real Stoic will probably shy away from being labeled as such.

You identify a Stoic by the silence that exudes from his being and the fire that radiates from his eyes. He is not one to possess a vacant look or a distressed countenance. In the harshest of situations, you will still find the man pensive and alert, and at no time will he lose control of his mind or his senses. He can be effectively forceful when he needs to be, and forgiving when the time is right.

Chapter 2

Perception of a Stoic

A Stoic's perception of everything around him and beyond his time and space is rather different than anything most people perceive. The human ability to perceive our surroundings and the events that occur around us is determined by a cornucopia of factors, ranging from how we were raised to how we see ourselves to what we expect to achieve and even some more convoluted structures of perception. But perception in itself is wrong because Stoics do not perceive—well, at least they endeavor over a lifetime to be able to see things as they are, rather than to perceive them through assumptions, presumptions, and experience.

To begin to see the truth, you need to let go of assumptions and perceptions. When you do, you will start to train the mind that you use to see things as they are and not the way you analogize them to be.

The journey as Stoics is an interesting one because we observe things in a new light each time we are faced with them. When we see a cloud, we see a cloud, not the white bunny, a choo-choo train, or any other associations that we tend to apply to things that are obviously not any of those things.

A Stoic sees a cloud for what it is, and that helps him to realize that it is neither good nor bad, but just the visible manifestation of water vapor.

We all know that perception is a function of knowledge, and that knowledge becomes the basis for our perception because our mind works by association. That's how we learn and assimilate information. What happens when you are fed information that is extremely alien? Most people take the elements of the topic, memorize the data, and then look for the relationship between the data in ways that are familiar. That is the process of understanding. If you think about it, memorization of data and understanding of the topic are two very different things. If you throw in accuracy of observation, and then interpretation of what is being observed, and on top of that you throw in the natural bias that each person possesses, then what you have is an almost unique interpretation of an event, even though everyone saw it and heard it at exactly the same moment.

The Stoic understands that perception and observation are key to the way he assimilates information and data. To get an idea of this, you need to understand the brain and how it works. Two things about the human brain require a cursory understanding.

The first is that the brain is separate from the five

senses that each of us possess. Your sight is a sense. That sense picks up light and converts it into an electric pulse that travels to the brain—specifically, it travels to the visual cortex. If what you are looking at happens to be accompanied by sound—let's say an explosion—then the sound that your ears detect travels to your auditory cortex.

But let's dissect it for a moment. Light and sound travel at different speeds. Light travels at 300 million meters per second, while sound travels at approximately 300 meters per second (actually it's 343 m/s). Light and sound travel at very different speeds, a million times different. If you stand 300 million meters away from an event that produces light and sound, the light will hit your eyes one second after the event. The sound from that same event will arrive at your ears a million seconds later (approximately). That's 11.5 days later. This is fact.

The minuscule time differences that exist between the perception of the event are certain. If you are standing a mile away from an explosion, the sight of that explosion will hit your eyes a fraction of a second earlier than the sound hits your ears. But in most cases, they always seem to happen at the same time. Why?

That's the brilliance of the way our brain is designed. The event of the explosion is broken down into two separate events—sight and sound, for the purpose of the brain's processing. The visual cortex processes the sight and then sends it to the hippocampus, while the auditory cortex sends what it has already processed to the hippocampus as well. The hippocampus then takes those two separate streams of information and stitches it together before passing it to your conscious self. That is why, for events close enough together, you see it as one seamless event.

When you get into a situation when there are multiple sounds and sights and your senses are overloaded, the hippocampus can't stitch things together in a way that makes sense and your conscious self-freezes because it can't get sufficient input to conjure a response—and you freeze. That's one of the strategies SWAT teams use to disorient their subjects by launching smoke, flash bombs, and creating loud noises. It totally discombobulates the target who can't respond to the invading team.

The point of bringing this up is to illustrate that the mind is designed to make up things if and when it knows that it needs to bridge the gap to make things right. You can't possibly be looking at an explosion and then experience the sound a split second later. It would become hectic to process multiple facets of the same event in the conscious mind. So the brain doesn't allow that, and it develops the ability to fill in the blanks and stitch up the delays.

What has all this to do with the Stoic's perception?

The Stoic understands the difference between observation and perception. He understands that observation can be clouded by a number of factors, not least of which is the limitations of the physical, mechanical, and temporal characteristics of all things. And he understands that this is just the start.

To put it simply, the Stoic knows that what he observes is not necessary what is actually happening. He understands that because our senses are limited by physical properties, the mind needs to bring in logic and reflection.

It doesn't end at just physical perception; it also is a function of physical perspective. A cube, when viewed from any of its sides, looks like only a square. Change the angle a little and look at it from a diagonal position and you see what could be a cube or a pyramid. You can't get the full understanding that it is a cube until you rotate the object and see the side that was initially unobservable. At this point, the whole picture is re-formed in your head and you know that it is a cube.

There is an ancient story that talks about seven blind men who were introduced to an elephant for the very first times in their lives. Each blind man was placed at a different spot around the animal and was asked to observe as much as he could and then report back.

The first blind man, who was placed at the trunk, expounded with certainty that the elephant was like a large snake. The man who was placed by its ears scoffed and said it was more like a large bat, to which the man placed at the belly of the beast scolded the first two and said the elephant was like a large wall. And so the differing opinion went around, with the man at the legs saying it was like a tree, and the man at the tail saying that it was like a little snake, and so on. None of them could agree, and they all left the scene in disagreement.

There are three things in this story that you should take away today. The first is that each man's perspective is unique and while it doesn't show the whole story, it shows the whole story to him. It is very hard to tell him otherwise once he has witnessed what he thinks is the truth.

The second is that what we always think we understand has deeper layers and nuances that will only become apparent if we take the time to walk around the elephant and hear the opinions of others.

Finally, the third is that we should never be so stubborn as to think that we know it all, or be so uncertain of ourselves that the first time someone tells us that something is not what we think, we fall apart in our conclusions.

The Stoic knows that his perception is only a starting

point and so he uses his logic to take the observations deeper. In time, that becomes a habit—you will see in later chapters that we talk more about habit and decision paths.

Decisions are the product of a path that we take. Stoics have a very well-defined path in their decision-making process and in time, with practice, that ability builds on itself. Stoics keep bias and prejudice out of the perception stage because that taints the starting point and determines the path.

You will be hard-pressed to find a Stoic, a true Stoic, who is loyal to anything or anyone more than they are loyal to the higher truth. They realize, as should you, that just because you see something doesn't make it the truth; there are more things at play than just the things you observe with your senses. A Stoic knows deeply that observations by the senses are just the starting point and that before they can respond there are more things that need to be included in their decision path.

Lesser minds are convinced that what they see is the only truth there is—have you noticed how conspiracy theories fester in the less educated minds?—or in the mind with the longest journey towards the mind of a Stoic.

Overthinking and deep thinking are two different things. You can't be accused of overthinking when you think deeply because overthinking highlights your biases, prejudices, and fears, while deep thinking removes them. That is the key difference between the two, and the Stoic is clearly a deep thinker, not an overthinker.

We need to take this further so that we can understand the circular nature of perception and reflection. To do that we need to jump in and look at reflection—the Stoic's tool to learn and extend his conscious abilities.

Reflection

A lot has been written about reflection and the power of thought that it magnifies. But as Stoics go, reflection is, yet again, a much richer and concentrated experience. The typical reflection you read about is like peach juice—a couple of peaches squeezed and bottled with the addition of syrups and added flavoring; the Stoic's reflection is more like top-shelf peach brandy—the fruits of 12 crates squeezed, then distilled and boiled till they thicken, then aged till the flavors naturally come out from them—not a drop of additive or flavor to enhance what is already present.

Reflection is not just the replaying of one's memories. It is also not the judgment of what happened based on your own experience (especially when that experience causes bias). Let's start with the first thing you shouldn't do. Most people start off reflection by going over an event in their minds. They especially choose the events that disturb them so that they can go over them in their heads and make sure that they don't happen again, or because they want to find a reason to lock onto and release the worry or sorrow they are feeling about that event. They search for reason, and in the process, beat themselves up for it. This is not reflection. In fact, it is the thing that you should not do, and it actually distracts you from living your life and completely sets you up on the path that precludes real reflection.

Instead, what you should do is look at all the things that happen in your life and in the lives of those around you. You are looking for the strain of commonality in all things and you are looking for the nature of how things unfold. In essence, you do not just look at the things that disturb you but also at the things that please you, and the things that you are indifferent to.

Stoics reflect on a daily basis. They do so in a form that is different from meditation—although their reflection can be meditative, their meditation is never reflective. Learn to appreciate that difference. When a Stoic descends into reflection, he clears his mind and instructs it to see the events in a neutral light so that he understands the events as they happened and not as he hopes, wishes, or mistakes them to have been. This is the first point. While he does that he also analyzes the nature of a person and the nature of his responses. He learns why he does certain things and why he didn't think of doing something differently. He looks at other ways of handling it and he looks for reason and logic.

A good way to break this down is to look at each action individually and query its reason for manifesting. Look at the initiating action and the way the responses unfolded. Take it one step at a time and compartmentalize each sub-event. Look at them individually, then look at them holistically. While you are doing this never dwell on issues or feel sorry for yourself or the other person. This is a time to dissect matters, test hypotheses, and learn for future events.

Finally, lay each issue to rest at the end of the reflection and chart a path of how you need to handle the subsequent unfolding of this action. You also should make a note of how to improve upon the outcome and upon yourself. Learn about the person you are dealing with and observe each tone, twitch, and point raised and you will get to know that person well. You will also learn to observe all things around you from what is said to how it is being said, and you will find, as Stoics do, that what is said is only half the picture in every conversation—how it is said completes the picture because a person can control what they say, but they can't control their body language.

Reflection is a solemn event. You are not here to smile and make jokes about what has happened—no matter how pleasing or funny. When you reflect, you are in a classroom and your teacher is the event that just transpired. An event is something that contains your presence, and the existence of all things around you, including the intangible of what was said, done, and thought. Everything that happens in and around you is your teacher for that moment you spend in reflection, and just like any good student, you should let the teacher speak to you, then return with questions.

Stoics have sometimes been thought of as heartless because they do not let anything bother them. They are not heartless, they are just cerebral, and they can be relied on to make the right decision when push comes to shove.

Real-time Effects of Reflection

When you reflect, there are a number of things that happen, and you will notice them within a few weeks. The first is that you will make it a habit. When it becomes a habit, then reflection, and the path it takes in the course of your session, will start to yield better results.

When you train your mind to look at things reflectively, it starts to become a habit as well and the mind changes its real-time thinking patterns as well. What you will notice is that your ability to evaluate your present situation gets better and starts yielding better outcomes. Better analysis, better execution, followed by better results, comes from real-time skills that reflection seems to produce. Think about it this way. Imagine you sit down in the comfort of your home without the pressures that the actual situation may have had and you take the time to look through each act, reaction, and consequence. Now imagine your ability to do the same thing while the act is live. Don't you think you will end up being a better decision maker? Of course you will. You can do that, with a little practice.

When you see a Stoic in action, what do you think he is doing when he looks preoccupied or looks unemotional? He is that way because, while everyone else is vacant in their thoughts, he is tapping into the benefit of reflection while the event is going on.

That is one of the powers of a Stoic that many people do not seem to understand or appreciate. They only see the Stoic's stoic façade and misunderstand the true meaning underneath it all. But the Stoic is not interested in niceties; he is interested in the truth of the moment—which requires him to capture all the streams of data flowing around him. The face that you see is the face of peace and contemplation—not indifference.

This chapter is about perception of the Stoic and yet we talk about reflection exhaustively. Before we go on with more methods of the Stoic's reflection and how that ties in with his perception, I want you to take a moment to understand the true linkage between perception, reflection, and the assimilation of information.

This will help you in a number of ways. It will help you become better at assessing any situation you find yourself, whether it is when you are flying a plane at 41,000 feet and encounter an emergency or are at home when a tsunami hits. How you apply your mind during periods of high data input—otherwise known as stressful situations—determines how far you go in life and in what direction. Suboptimal lives are hardly ever the result of bad situations, but rather, the consequence of bad decisions on how to react to those situations.

A Stoic lives by the ideal that there is no good or bad. Remember that. A Stoic sees only consequence and the long horizon. A decision that has a good outcome now but has a poor outcome in the longer term is not something the Stoic will chose.

That in itself turns back around and influences the perception that he has. Since he doesn't see the situation as bad, but only the possible reaction that he has to it, guess who is in control of his destiny? Yes, that's right, he, the Stoic, is the one with the control of how things unfold for himself. When you place the responsibility for the outcome on your own shoulders, you have the power to do anything because you are no longer thinking about fate or luck.

The Stoic does not use the excuse of bad luck or the hope for good luck in his deliberations and reflections. A Stoic makes his own luck, so to speak. He does not hope that something improbable will happen just to make things right for him.

When you have this sort of frame of mind, you end up making the effort necessary to be in the state that is required to absorb the surroundings and refrain from being mistakenly corralled into conclusions that are tinted by less than all the facts. The truth, not just what is visually discernable, is the Stoic's tool, and because what you see is not always what is true, you have to apply the necessary thinking to understand something. That is the reason the Stoic must reflect all the time. The mind is the third dimension in the pursuit of the truth. Why? Because, as you will see in Chapter 5, the way the mind works with the senses, we cannot always just rely on what we see because it is not always correct.

Let me give you an example of why that is so.

When scientists looked into space, the smartest of the lot at the time (we are talking about the days before Einstein) agreed that space was a vacuum and there was nothing in it. The space between the planets was filled with a void, and so was the rest of the universe. According to them, there was a whole lot of nothing. We now know that space is filled with something called Dark Matter.

Can you take a guess why it is called Dark Matter? You will love this. It's because it is dark to us and we can't see it and so we call it dark. Makes sense, but it also shows you something interesting about the nature of humans and the way we acquire knowledge.

The reason for that was because we could not detect the elements of space—and thus we called it that—space (as in empty space) But we now know that just because we can't detect it doesn't mean that it does not exist. Science has sometimes faltered in its pursuit because science is so disciplined that it can only believe what it can prove, and it can only prove what it observes; all else is considered non-existent. Do you see the mess that this can cause?

Dark Matter can't be detected by us without the use of specialized equipment, and that equipment has not been developed yet. So how do we know it is there? We see it with our minds. That really does deserve further expounding.

When you have the mind of a Stoic, you use your mind to see things that your eyes can't see—No, I don't mean that you hallucinate. I mean that you understand with your mind something that your senses can't detect. So you see it with your mind's eye.

We can't see Dark Matter because we had no need to see it for our survival and so nothing that could be detected and used entered our evolutionary development. Visible electromagnetic radiation prompted the development of our eyes, mechanical sound waves prompted the development of our ears, and temperature senses developed to trigger our homeostasis reflexes so that we can adapt to the changing temperatures we are subjected to from one moment to the next. Everything that evolved in us came about because we needed it to navigate this world. Dark Matter was not one of these things, and so we can't detect it—that does not mean that it is not there.

One of the ways you can develop this mind's eye is by reflecting. The more you reflect, the more you teach your mind the way things are, and that allows it to plot scenarios and think of ways to do things. The more the Stoic reflects, the more his mind's eye develops, and that allows him to have an almost omnipresent ability.

Perception

This brings us back full circle to perception. Once you know your basic perception is incomplete, you start to enhance it with your mind and what was once basic input grows to be more sophisticated. That is the Stoic's ability: to perceive things that most people would just not even know to look for.

So let's look at perception again. Perception is not just

the information that we receive from our senses; it is also the stitching together of the events using the mind—how well we stitch them together and how much we open our minds to see more deeply is up to us. But it requires practice and determination to put in the effort to not just take in the information passively but to parse it, actively scan for it, unemotionally absorb it, and efficiently aggregate it to get the whole picture.

Some things we get from unwitting experience while others we get from tenacious persistence in the pursuit of the truth. The truth is not as simple as breathing air. It takes the combination of many aspects, including the five senses and cogitation, before it can appear. Those who only believe what they see with their eyes are easily fooled. To test that theory you only have to watch one of the many magic shows that are on TV. Many of them are so obvious, but the slow mind is unable to catch them. We all have the same pair of eyes; the difference lies in the way we see things. Some choose to see things in a simple way; others overcomplicate it. Whatever it is, the way we see things will change once we start spending time reflecting on the day's events every day until the thought process of the reflection becomes a habit that is used during real-time events.

Whether you realize it, Einstein was not really a scientist in the traditional sense of the word. He was a Stoic. And by that I don't mean it as a religion. Stoicism is as much a religion as the Pledge of Allegiance is a prayer. Stoicism is not something you get inducted into like the Masons or baptized into like a religion. It is not even something you swear into, like taking a citizenship oath.

Chapter 3

The Character of a Stoic

What is character? Is it based on your beliefs? Or is it based on your view of yourself? Could it be the sum of all your experiences mirrored back onto society? What exactly do you think of when someone utters the term?

Whether you are just getting started on your path to Stoicism or you are investigating it because you heard of it, I want you to know that the purpose of this book is to come as close as possible to showing you the start of the path to the practice and status of this discipline.

Stoicism is not a religion or an allegiance. It is a state that you are in. No one can force you into this state, and you cannot decide to be Stoic just because you like what it represents. Being Stoic is about the fabric that makes up who you are, not the dye or the stitching that comes on top of it. However you train, or whatever you read or study, doesn't serve to change that fabric. It only removes the stains and dust that may have accumulated on top of it. In essence you are either a Stoic in nature, or you are not; your journey is about finding it within, not learning it from without.

In the last chapter, we looked at perception and

reflection. We looked at how reflection fosters better perception, and if you carry that further you will see that better perception carries better reflection as well. So what you get is a spiraling rise in perceptive powers and that leads to solid intuition.

When you get to that point, it starts to have an overflow effect on a person and the world around them. As you pick up momentum what you see is a change and improvement in your character. Two things in particular happen—the first is that you see a person that is more cerebral, and the second is that you see a person of character.

We are going to spend much of this chapter laying the ground work on the character of the Stoic so that the last chapter on his perception makes more sense in this light, and the following chapters on minimalism, and later, on discipline, then on meditation, form a complex interplay of symphonic proportions.

When you attend the symphony—and I have to just say that it is one of my favorite things to do because it is just an out of this world/out-of-body experience—you walk in, and by the time you leave, you've been changed somehow.

The beauty of the symphony is that its complexity is never-ending. That is the quality of the Stoic's character. Under scrutiny, the Stoic's character keeps yielding layers of nuance that seems inhuman. It even comes across in their writing. Again, if you haven't already, you should read Marcus Aurelius' *Meditations*. After a dozen reads you start to see the complexity of the man and the life that he describes when you embrace life as a Stoic. Just when you think it doesn't get any simpler than this, WHAM, it hits you and you fall deeper into a renewed sense of profound amazement of life, nature, and the universe.

I was once told that the best teacher is not the man who teaches incessantly, but the man who quietly and effortlessly exhibits all that a student should learn.

What is your definition of character? Is it something that resides deep within a man's soul? Or could it be that character is a set of guidelines on how to act, such as which fork to use for the salad for good manners? Are these a projection of character?

Or is character something more? Indeed, if you think that character is the essence of a person, then you are on the right track. Character is the taste of oak in the sip of a perfectly brewed tea. It is so deep inside that it can only be detected by the mind but not by the senses.

Coming back to the symphony, a man's character is comprised of the full complement of percussions, woodwinds, strings, and brass that competently navigate the various movements of the symphony with ease to deliver a stunning and life-altering experience.

A Stoic's character, as you can tell by now, is

unconventional and complex, but it is not that way for that purpose. In other words, he is not complex because he wants to be seen that way or he wants to be perceived that way. He is not the kind of person that sees himself through the eyes of others. Most people, non-Stoics that is, see themselves through the eyes of those around them—from the eyes of those they love to the eyes of those they hate. Depending on their internal demons the scale teeters between the two sides. If a person is typically driven by anger, then the people that he hates defines the character of that man. If the person is driven by love, then his character is driven by the perception of those he loves.

Before we proceed we need to take that one step up. It is not just the people who love or hate him that draw this picture; it goes one step further. It is really about what a person thinks those people think of him—stop there for a minute. Look at that for a minute. When a man's character is driven by those he hates or those he loves, it is actually driven by his imagination of what those people think. That is unhealthy and it is not something a Stoic even participates in. He is never worried about what others think of him and what others say of him. He has a higher loyalty to the higher truth and if that seems to clash with the people around him, then it is of no concern to him. This makes his character unassailable.

It also frees up his mind. Can you imagine the amount

of brainpower it takes to keep altering your trajectory just so that you can keep up with the impressions and thoughts of others? In essence, that is what one does when one's character is driven by the thoughts of others. It's like a politician before the election: on one day he wears one face to please one demographic and the next day he is another. It consumes so much that you can't do anything—including reflect like you should to fortify your understanding of the world around you. It is a dangerous course to plot.

The first thing about a Stoic's character is that it is his own. A Stoic's character is formed and forged by the pursuit of truth and peace. Remember, a Stoic is not in a popularity contest and so he is free to adhere to the morals of longevity. The morals of longevity describe the actions of morality that have a timeless horizon.

The Morals of Longevity

Morals are not something that you learn in civics class or something that you can accomplish by merely reading a textbook. It takes a long hard road in this immoral world to ferret out and distinguish what morals are and how they fit with your own sensibilities.

A cursory look at history shows that even morals and fortitude are defined by the prevailing generation and they follow the rule of the pendulum in that they swing from one extreme to the next. Morals can't be defined by democracy, and history tells us this repeatedly. But the moral of the Stoic—from great men like Seneca, Plutarch, and the Emperor himself—has been one that has been able to stand the onslaught of time and progress.

The Stoic does not define the morals that guide him by the flavor of the period but rather by deep introspection and study. It is a fine balance of lessons learned and experiences gained that the Stoic sets as the compass of his moral machinery.

You can too.

If you are expecting to find a set of codes and teachings that will help you set your moral compass, I am sorry to disappoint. It doesn't work that way. Morals are distilled from experience and reflection upon generations of thought leaders and philosophers that went before us and did not spell out a series of guidelines, but rather provided narratives and parables. Take Plato's account of Socrates' life and death. There is no single guide or commandment to memorize, but yet the whole narrative goes to paint a picture that rewards those who really pay attention. Stoics read books and pamphlets like these, though their lives are in order, to gain insight into worthy observations of men in the past. Even though we live life where we can fly faster than the speed of sound or reach other planets, the essence of the human soul remains the same. Our bodies and ideals may have evolved, but our souls remain untouched and so the lessons in life that applied to one generation long ago can still apply to us today.

There are lessons everywhere. Remember, your morals are like the Constitution that sits at the center of all else within you. It is like the American Constitution. Any law that is created can be tested against the Constitution and if it fails to adhere to those laws, they are struck down and superseded by the Supreme Court's ruling. In the same way, you may have ideals and principles that you pick up along the way and they may hold for some time. But if you test them against this set of morals and they don't add up, then these other actions and beliefs that you picked up need to be discarded.

Your morals are your own. Your morals are not just your code of conduct. They are your life raft when the floods arrive. The Stoic's character is a mix of all things that you have read in this book and obit the moral code that they live by. By this point you know that the Stoic is in pursuit of peace and truth. His moral code works to promote that, and it also works in reverse as well.

Peace and truth also define the Stoic's moral code. It is also tested for its longevity which means that the morals must not be something that suits a momentary horizon. Higher truths are higher because they are timeless and do not lend themselves to be swayed by momentary lapses in collective behavior. Stoics are never swayed by the mood of the populace. They, in fact, are the anchors of the human potential.

When you develop your own morals or you test their efficacy, your first test should be to test it for longevity. That should be your first step.

The Humility of Omniscience

A Stoic who has practiced reflection and meditation will develop an air of invincibility. His morals, which give mass to his character, are not ones that are superficial, and they can't be faked. But that strength is magnified even further by the humility that he possesses. That humility is not a practiced visage, it is a true brand of knowing that his knowledge gives him strength and he does not need to display arrogance to show his ability. The flames of his humility is famed by is almost perfect omniscience.

So your next question is surely about how to develop the omniscience of a Stoic. Well, we have already covered that. It comes from reflection. Reflection is such a powerful process in a Stoic's life, and it is not something that is exclusive or expensive. It only requires that you pay attention and that you are mindful of the things that are going on around you. When you are in the privacy of your own space then you can look back at all the events that transpired along the multiple data streams that you were aware of during the event, and you then learn from there. In time, that internalizes, and your grasp of things becomes nothing short of clairvoyant.

The point of this section is to underscore the humility of the Stoic, not his omniscience. The reason this is underscored is because there are others out there who are also highly intelligent and border on having uncommon awareness, but they lack the crowning characteristic needed to round out the picture and that is humility.

The characteristic of humility is not a one-way street. You don't just pay it forward. Humility is not about them, it is about you. When you are humble, it magnifies your ability to detect and appreciate the truth. The moment you allow arrogance to take hold, it erodes your Stoic character like the Colorado carving the Grand Canyon.

So humility not only comes from knowing everything and having the desire to know more, it is also the ladder to higher truths. So it is a spiral, once again, where one thing leads to another and that leads to more understanding.

The humility of a Stoic is legendary. Stoics are forceful when they need to be, but that is draped in humility so that they can maintain their even keel, and their character projects that in all that they do.

In essence, foster humility and it will serve you well in your enlightenment; advance your enlightenment and find that you realize that what you know you know is a fraction of what you know you don't know—and that instantly dress you up in humility.

Chapter 4

Minimalism of a Stoic

Before we get into the idea of minimalism within the context of a Stoic, it is worth noting that minimalism in the general sense doesn't quite apply to the Stoic. New Age discussion looks at minimalism as the noble forgoing of comforts and possessions. You see that everywhere that a higher truth is sought and you see that in the quest for a meditative life. But the thing that is most distinct about the way a Stoic sees it is that minimalism is not about forgoing material possession or choosing silence over clutter. A Stoic embraces minimalism, but that minimalism is about internal disassociation that then prevents distraction.

Put it this way—a minimalist believes that he shouldn't own a sports car; a Stoic believes there is nothing wrong with the car, as long as it is not going to raise the fire of his ego or obscure the perspective of truth. That's the first difference. There is more.

A minimalist, in the New-Age definition, sees life as a series of events that tame the demands of the flesh. Their contention, and it has merit for a part of society, is that limiting the distractions of the flesh allows the mind to develop its full potential. The Stoic has forgone the sensations and the sway of the flesh. In other words, the former looks at minimalism as the way to quell the chaos of the flesh so that the mind's whisper can be heard; the latter has already conquered the self and is in tune with the mind. One needs minimalism to find his way and, as such, defines it accordingly; the other lives minimalism and doesn't need the outward action to hear his mind.

Let's take a granular look at it. To do that, we need to see and understand the mind and being of the human being.

There are three parts of us. First, there is the body—and it is a huge part of what we do and even how we think. Second, there is the mind. The mind is able to do numerous things—all of which are intangible. Our mind is hugely influenced by the opinion and input of the body. It consists of multiple dimensions including one that is conscious and another that is—and by that I hardly mean that it is asleep or comatose. It is an amazing organ with chemical, biological, electrical, and even quantum aspects to it. Finally, there is the intangible aspect of the interaction between the body and the mind and that results in a sequence of behavior that would not exist if the mind did not need to deal with the input of the body or if the body had no mind to contend with.

For all intents and purposes, it is easier to separate the body and the mind and look at them as adversaries battling over a point in court. The advocate for the body, fighting for bodily instincts, and the advocate for the mind, fighting for learned guidelines. Take eating, for instance. Eating is a bodily instinct. The body needs you to eat so that it can energize and replenish itself, but the mind reminds you that you can't eat too much even though you feel like it and you are rewarded with bliss for carrying it out.

We've all been through that: when we feel like we want to do one thing but we also think we shouldn't. The two sides of us being torn apart and, more often than not, until it is resolved our external self languishes in indecision. There is one way of coping with that, but it requires the understanding and execution of discipline—that is the topic of the next chapter.

But for now we need to just look at the duality that exists within us and it is that duality that gives rise to the successes and the mistakes each of us make every day of our lives—and sometimes we pass that on to the next generation and then it continues with those mistakes or those habits.

The duality in each of us is the third aspect of the individual. Think about it this way. On one side you have black, and on the other side you have white (do not read into black and white being good and bad—it is just an example) at the point where they intersect you get gray. That it is the third aspect of your being—the amalgamation and the contradiction of the two sides. It is not always in opposition, and it is not always in unison; it is not always in the same degree of union and opposition—as such you get a certain character profile that builds from there. That's where we live—in that area of gray between the pull of the mind and the pull of the body.

Up to this point in this chapter we have been painting a picture with analogies. I urge you to keep that in mind and travel the path of the analogy to a limited extent, just enough to take you where you need to be to see the truth of this within yourself.

Let's get back to the duality and third aspect of yourself.

In actual fact, all the battles that happen do so in your brain—albeit different parts of your brain. The bodily instinct—the so-called "flesh" in the analogy—is typically located in the ancient part of the brain close to the base and the center. The base of the brain that is really the central nervous system is the evolutionary start of what eventually grew to be the brain. This base is where the instincts of survival reside—you can think of them as a hardwired code of survival. This part of the brain has an underlying task which is to survive and prolong the species. Fear, anger, hunger, reproduction, and all the primal instincts you can think of are driven and controlled by this half of the brain.

The other half (I do not intend to use the term half to

denote any measure or volumetric inference) is merely to describe the two sides of the opposing forces in the brain.

Separating the Body from the Mind

The Stoic understands that the body's inclinations and urges are not a bad thing and are not something to feel guilty about. There is no right and wrong in a Stoic's mind because he understands very clearly that the battle between the two sides results in one of three outcomes.

Every action a person takes is either one that the mind has enforced, one the body has enforced, or the languishing action of indecision. When one is a child the instinct portion of the brain is strong and has sway over the person's actions. Most adults forgive the child as they know that they have yet to mature and they spend a good part of the first decade watching the kid get the basics. Then the mind starts to wake up and the conflict between the mind and the "body" start to occur more frequently. You start to see the kid gripped by indecision more often than he was previously—this typically defines the teenage years, or at least the early parts of them. The events and confusion during that stage of life are a harbinger of the way most adults treat life later on. Stoics grow out of that. And that is one way to look at the life of a Stoic—it is the life of a well-adjusted adult, vacant of bias and impulses.

In many cases, much of society has found that the errors we make in life are ones that come from the urge to satisfy the impulses of the body. For instance, the need to have a rich life—(wealth bestows security) and the desire to do nothing (laziness conserves energy) results in a person who might cheat and steal—always trying to get something for nothing. That's what cheaters and con-men are—impulsive to satisfy their desires but unwilling or unable to put in the work. A Stoic hardly gets into that problem because, by definition, the Stoic has his impulses in check. That usually doesn't work out so well and they end up spending most of their life avoiding consequences that arise from poor decision-making.

Minimalists, in the traditional sense, are not wrong in their intentions or in the way they go about them. What are those intentions? Well, those intentions are about settling the debate between the primal and the modern side of the brain.

Let me draw you a picture. Have you ever fasted? If you haven't, you should. It is an amazing experience and it goes a long way in developing the state you need to be in as a Stoic, but more on that later. When you fast for the first time (and maybe a few times after that), you will typically feel hunger which will then slowly descend into a sense of despair. All these are sensations that your primal brain (what we typically like to call the body or the flesh) triggers to get your attention and are forms of negative reinforcement; that sensation of doom gets your mind to imagine the worst. People fasting for the first time inevitably think that they will starve or cause irreparable damage to their body. What's more insidious is the sensation that makes you feel that it is pointless. Whatever you're feeling is being conjured up from within you and it's not what you think it is. And therein lies the lesson in fasting. Once you overcome those feelings, you start to acquire the ability to distinguish what is real from what your primal brain is telling you. Your primal brain was built to survive and it does that by eating. Once you choke that off, the primal brain tries everything in its power to make that decision of yours as uncomfortable as possible.

On the other hand, your intellectual side knows that you can't possibly starve and die with just a 24-hour fast, and so what really happens is that you start to recognize the voice of doubt that the primal mind plants in you. This is supremely beneficial because that voice of hesitance, the tremor of doubt, and the fear of doom, all sound suspiciously the same. When you train yourself to detect that voice, you start to identify the players. When you start to identify the players, you start to understand their pattern. That's when you start to make better decisions. It's not that fasting makes you a stronger person, it's that it introduces you to your demons; and once you know them, then their methods are familiar to you so that you can avoid them in all other situations as well. The pull of the body can be hard to resist and you need practice. You can't walk up to 200-pound weights and bench press them the first time you set foot in a gym. You need to work at it and get to the point where your body has the power and stamina to move the weight against the force of gravity and your mind has evidence that it can be done and has the ability to do it. In the same way, minimalism shows you that you can survive without having to feed your ego.

Minimalism and Fasting

This is where minimalism comes in as well. It does the same thing that fasting does. When you embrace minimalism as a rule, you are introduced to a number of phenomena. The first is that you are introduced to your ego—the part of you that wants to have things for the sake of showing others that you have them. It's like the art collector who buys branded art to show others he has it but doesn't actually understand what he is buying. Or the guy who buys designer shoes for the brand value but has no appreciation for the quality, workmanship, and depth of the product.

These are the people who need minimalism to exhibit to them the voice of the ego and for them to catch on to the fact that their true strength comes from their intellectual side and their ego has no part it in. In fact, it could be a stumbling block. A person who thinks he needs to be branded from head to toe, so that he can project an air of success, is going to project an air of failure when he doesn't have all those things. You will never see that in a Stoic. Most Stoics are successful in their own right and do not need external airbrushing to project who they are.

Let's get back to the generic minimalism. You should have an idea by this point what minimalism is supposed to import. It's quite simple, really—it is an amazing tool to hone your senses, just as fasting does, and it gets you to chisel off all the unnecessary clinging to things and clutter that tends to distract you from what you are really capable of and the false rewards and comforts that only place obstacles in your mind.

For the uninitiated, minimalism does one more thing: it unleashes your hunger so you see what's happening is that, on one hand, you are teaching your body that the lesson hardwired in your genes can be overridden. But at the same time you are unleashing the power that comes online when you have nothing.

Minimalism is a powerful tool, but the misunderstanding that comes from those who don't know what comes next results in a wide swath of New-Age believers thinking that minimalism is the end game. It is not.

Minimalism is the beginning. When you get used to minimalism you are free to achieve anything without thinking about the reward that is uncertain. You rewire your brain to face a new reality that transcends the short-term gain. When you do this, you force the brain to stop calculating the risk-to-reward ratio, or the effort to reward ratios that it inherently calculates for everything that you do.

How many times have you wanted to do something but haven't had the motivation to get up and do it and are told that you need to take it step by step? The reason you need to take it step by step is so that you can provide proof to the brain that the incremental steps toward the big goal are possible. It works, and that is because your brain is used to calculating effort to reward. The brain is a super economic calculator. It looks at your input factors and then your possible outcome and determines whether you should be motivated to do what is necessary. That is the formula for survival.

I love observing nature and watching powerful beasts in their element. You will see this economic calculation in full display. Cheetahs are the fastest land animals on earth. That speed that they unleash on a prey, coupled with their ability to focus, anticipate, and pounce on wildebeests makes their effort pay off almost every time. And they have to make sure it pays off because the speed that they unleash requires a tremendous amount of energy output and if they do not eat after a chase—meaning they fail in their attempt—it could result in depletion of energy reserves. If that happens more than once or twice, the cheetah faces starvation and exhaustion. To avoid this, the cheetah instinctively calculates its move and its attack. If it finds that its attempt won't be successful, it won't even try.

Humans are cut from the same cloth—in fact, so are all living creatures. We are hardwired to not even attempt something if our internal economist does not believe the payoff is almost certain. So we have learned to find ways around that because the original intent of the effort vs payoff equation doesn't hold anymore. We do not need to hunt our meals. We don't need to expend so much energy and effort to get our next meal, yet the instinct still persists. Except now it's not food that we need to expend effort and energy for; we need to expend it for the reward.

That idea of calculating the reward and putting the effort forth for that reward is never a good idea in today's world because it results in mediocre outcomes. Once you remove the reward from the equation, then your body readjusts and you realize that the pattern of your pursuits has changed.

That's what minimalism is supposed to do. It is the dumbbells that lead to the 200-pound bench press. Minimalism is boot camp for endeavors that will result in outcomes we are unable to fathom until they are successful. Look at Edison and the light bulb, Gates and Microsoft, Jobs and Apple. If any one of those people looked at the effort and tried to compare it to an outcome that they had no idea of, they would have given up even before taking the first step.

What does all this have to do with minimalism, and more appropriately, what does it have to do with Stoic minimalism?

Well, all that we have looked at in the last chapter has been a build-up to understanding the objective of minimalism—whether you are Stoic or not, minimalism is about the same thing. It is just approached and executed differently.

Curbing the Primal Mind

One more time—minimalism is designed to curb the vestiges of our primal mind in this modern world. It is important that we do this because the primal mind is designed to survive. And Stoics don't just survive, they thrive, and accomplish great feats that reverberate through the ages. That pull of the primal mind turns out to be one of the greatest distractions and retardants a man can face. The famous seven sins one reads about in Dante's Inferno, those that the major religions of the world define as sin, include gluttony, sloth, pride, envy, lust, greed, and wrath. The old folks tell us that these are the sins that will ruin us and that the devil inside us is the one causing all this. We are told to banish the devil and to embrace God in order to not be doomed to hell for all eternity.

It turns out that this advice is not bad. The sins that they are referring to are not really those of the devil, but those of the primitive mind, and they need to be tempered by the intellect. So what you see as sin today is actually the tools we needed to survive when we were in the stages of evolution. Without greed, we would not know when to hunt or when to eat or even be able to store food for a later date. Without lust, we would not have been able to advance the species. Without envy, we would not have been able to mimic our neighbors and do better for ourselves. Without sloth, we would not have been able to temper our enthusiasm and we would not have been able to manage our stores of energy. We would have chased after any old endeavor and wasted lots of energy on foolhardy ideas. Laziness tempered that. Imagine the cheetah chasing a rabbit and expending ten times the energy in the pursuit of that rabbit than it will get after consuming it—it's a net loss. But if the laziness algorithm in the cheetah is working well, it will look at the rabbit and say—"it's not worth it." Without anger, we would not be able to protect and defend ourselves. Get the picture? Our primal mind was hardwired with all these things based on the surrounding circumstances, and that was passed down to us via our genetic code. Those tools still have their uses and, if used correctly, can be beneficial. But what we need to do is find a way to make it more relevant and to do that we need to temper it and subject it to the will of the intellect.

That's what Stoicism is. It is the accomplishment of all that is necessary to bring the primal side of our self under control. So how does a Stoic see minimalism if not by the way the others see it?

Do not mistake one fact—a distraction is a distraction, regardless if you are a Stoic or otherwise. The difference is that the Stoic has already brought his seven sins under control and so doesn't need to perform the rituals needed on the outside to affect the self on this inside.

Minimalism, fasting, celibacy, vows of silence, and tithing are all ways we have found to combat each excess of the primal mind in different areas. Celibacy counters lust; minimalism counters greed; fasting counters gluttony, and so on. These ways to combat the excesses simply flex the intellectual muscles and the will to overcome what is instinctively rewarding. Once we learn to forgo that reward of the flesh, we don't need to take extreme measures. But while we are in the grips of it, we need discipline—which we will look at in the next chapter.

These are, of course, simplified greatly so that the

concept fits within the bounds of this book, but you get the point. It is simple and it is logical. If you have too much white paint, you add some black to get gray; if it gets too gray, then you add some white. Essentially, you use the opposing color to balance the color you have to get the color you want.

What does a Stoic want? The Stoic wants peace and truth. He can't get that with the primal instincts left unabated and screaming in the background, so he tempers all those instincts with the opposing factor and brings them all under control. Once those instincts are brought under control, it is easier to see things for what they are without fear or favor and to process them without the distraction of the primal. This achieves what the Stoic wants—peace and truth.

So how does the Stoic practice minimalism?

He does so very differently from the way non-Stoics do. Non-Stoics deprive themselves of physical things and clutter to cut down on the noise. Stoics cut off the effect of the physical things within their own mind. So it doesn't matter what is around them; it doesn't affect them at any level and that keeps them true to their need for peace and higher truth.

Here is how it works.

A Stoic knows that the Rolls Royce in his garage is there only for his refined taste, not because he wants to one-up his neighbor's Bentley or he wants to be seen so that adulations flow his way. He wants the refined leather and the exquisite stitching because they appeal to his demand for quality and precision. He is looking inward when he wants something; he is not looking outward at what others may say of him, and with that he peels away the first layer of the ego.

The Stoic's minimalism effect is in his mental realm, not in his physical one. Here is a thought exercise that you can conduct to see the difference. Wherever you are at this moment, assume it is in your home or room and you are surrounded by copious amounts of your things. Some things are there for vanity; some are there for identity; others are just there and have become a part of you. Now imagine giving it all away. For just one instant, imagine if the movers came and you instructed them to take it and give it all away. What would you be left with? Nothing. Only the tools you need to make a living. So if you are a mechanic, keep your wrenches and so on. If you are a software programmer, keep your laptop and computers. If you are an artist, keep your paint and brushes. Just keep the tools you need to make a living. Imagine how this would make you feel. Do you feel that emptiness? Is it impossible to consider that you no longer have all those photos, those gifts, those DVDs, or those comfy sheets to sleep on. But in the midst of all that, you have to come to the realization that you are still alive.

Some lament the photos of families, mementos from generations ago, hard-earned money spent on furniture, and now all gone. Now deal with that for a while until you come to the conclusion that you do not need all those things to make something of yourself. In fact, all those things were merely distractions. What you will face at this point is the sadness and the pain of giving all those things away because you identified with them; they were your security blanket, your reason for things, your rewards for accomplishment—they were a testament to who you are. But if you really think about it, you do not need any of those things to live. In fact, those things cause you to slow down. They hold you back and they cloud your thoughts.

As part of my personal journey, I once gave away all my possessions and only kept what could fit into one bag. It contained only the things that I needed to live decently—clothes, personal hygiene items, sleeping bag, iPad for work, and a few small tools. Everything from fridge to stove to toaster—everything went out the door. Even my car. For two and a half years I swore off all the luxurious comforts of life and just made do with what was necessary, and I found what I was looking for. I found my peace and my truth. When my mind was not distracted by all those things that I once engaged in, I was able to see things far more deeply than I ever had and it brought me to the path that saw things in ways that I was not equipped to do before I had rid myself of the distractions.

I no longer live a life of minimalism externally because I recognize what that looks like, and even in the midst of chaos I can still find the serene silence I need to enjoy peace and touch the truth of the moment. My earnings from my contributions to society are not rewards; the things I purchase do not make me vainglorious. I see the beauty of things for what they are and the utility of things for what they can do, and I have no misguided notion of what I need to project to someone who has no clue who I am in the hopes that he will think well of me.

The 30 months spent within my own mind, not caring about what others thought, changed my life. Moving away from external tokens that defined my true value and incorrectly measured my contribution changed the way I see myself, and that changed the way I valued myself. That in turn pushed me to a life of greater contribution—one where I don't need to determine if the reward is good enough.

But the Stoic doesn't need to physical extricate his being from the surrounding possessions to embrace the effect of minimalism—he can do it in his head. Some of us do it naturally, some do it intentionally, some need copious amounts of discipline to accomplish it, and so on. There are so many paths to get to the internal detachment of our spirit and the things around us.

What is important is that we can identify ourselves in the midst of distraction because we know what to look for. Have you ever been in a crowded room and you look around to find the love of your life? If you don't know what she looks like, you obviously won't find her. But if you already know her and she is in that room, you can pick her out of the crowd without even seeing her face. You will recognize her hair, her gait, her posture, and all the subtle things that will lock your gaze onto her.

In the same way, an exercise in minimalism will introduce you to the power of an undistracted state; it will lock your gaze onto your true self and what it feels like to be undistracted and uncluttered so that when you do inevitably bring on all those things into your life, they will no longer be distracting in nature, but rather, they will elevate you to a level that you can't imagine.

Minimalism to the Stoic is something that you can only experience and you really only need to do it once in your life to be able to latch onto it and realize that the benefit it has surpasses anything that you have previously experienced.

If you take people like Gates, Jobs and Buffet and you look at the way they see themselves, you can just get the feeling that with all those resources, they don't let any of the distractions get to them. A flight on the private jet is just a means of getting somewhere, not the arrogance of being airlifted in the lap of luxury. Designer shoes are not about a name branded to the heel, but rather the demand for exquisite workmanship. I have seen countless people impressed by the branding but blind to the workmanship. I have seen people respond in awe to the Spirit of Ecstasy symbolizing the Rolls Royce on the hood of the car but haven't seen anyone appreciate the attention to detail and craftsmanship that appeals to the Stoic.

It is possible to be a Stoic minimalist and still ride chauffeur-driven in a Rolls Royce, as long as you know how to separate the distraction from the appreciation. One will dim your light, the other will magnify it.

Chapter 5

The Discipline of a Stoic

One of the main tenets that guide the Stoic mind is a discipline that goes beyond the definitions that are usually attached to it. We define discipline in ways that seem medieval and harsh. We see discipline as something that is lacking and deserves punishment. We see discipline as the harder voice to the playful self. Our faulty idea of discipline and the eventual inability to invoke it puts us in the path of many consequences that distract and derail us, and so those who do master discipline manage to walk a hamstrung/straight jacket life.

But that is not the discipline we need, nor the discipline that Stoics practice. Stoic discipline is easy to institute because it is based on truth and reality. It is based on the understanding of our bodies and the habits of our minds.

This chapter will look at the discipline of the Stoic in its functional reality and entirety. It is the discipline you need to hold your values in check and in place to live a life that is peaceful, constructive, and useful.

In the last chapter we talked about minimalism and we

saw that in many cases, discipline plays a huge role in it. There are two forms of discipline that we need to be aware of. One discipline is the will of the mind over the body; the second discipline is the will of the mind over the mind. It can get pretty confusing but we will sort that out in this chapter.

We often get confused with the true nature of discipline. It's no wonder that that happens when that term has been repeatedly pounded into us in the classroom and living room. When we don't do what we must, we are accused of lacking discipline. When we do something we shouldn't, we are chided for not being disciplined. There are so many ways to use the word and none of them seem to be pleasant. It leaves us with this foul taste in our mouth, like penicillin without the protection of the dissolvable capsule.

But just like penicillin, it has its benefits—while the downside is merely superficial.

Let's erase all that and rekindle our association with this term.

Habits

We live our life in a time when the ghost of our evolutionary past makes some things difficult for us to do. We saw much of this in the last chapter, but that phenomenon shows up again here because it is a part of who we are.

Think of a habit. When you have a habit, it is a really a string of three things that happen. There is a cue, a response, and a reward. When you drive to work and you come to a stoplight, that instantly triggers the response of turning in the direction you need to proceed. Making the correct turn makes you feel that all is well in the world. If you make the wrong turn, you feel awful—negative reinforcement.

Let's look at something more. Let's say you smoke every day after a meal. As soon as you are done with your meal, the habit to light up is triggered, and that gives you, in addition to the nicotine, pleasure. You see the pattern—trigger, followed by response.

Everything forms some form of habit—even behavior, people (seeing someone, hearing their voice, and so on), things, experiences. Withdrawal is a negative habit. If you are used to one thing, even though you do not get the pleasure of seeing it or experiencing it, you will feel it in the event that it is absent. It is a category of habit that uses negative reinforcement.

These forces that act on you can have a debilitating effect and they can be a distraction. Smoking as a hobby is pleasant to enjoy; smoking to relieve a habit is a distraction. Gambling for the fun of it is invigorating, but gambling to satisfy a habit is a vice. Sex as part of a marriage can be necessitated by the desire to have offspring. Sex can also be for the enjoyment of pleasure. But sex that is demanded to satisfy a craving repeatedly is unhealthy.

We think of all these things in terms of balance. The need for food, in balance, is healthy. The greed for food, in abundance, is fatal.

Stoics are not prone to scratching an itch. They do things for the efficacy or for the enjoyment but they never allow it to control them. Any form of control over one's actions leads to unintended and negative consequences that in itself can be a distraction to things in the future. So, the execution of the act because of the need to satisfy this kind of habit erodes the strength of the mind and causes distractions in the present, and distraction in the future when the time comes to pay the piper.

Moderation in all you do is essential and to get the moderation going, you need a kind of discipline.

Let me illustrate.

I was raised as far back as I can remember to wake up at 5:30 a.m. There was no such thing as days off or on. It wasn't predicated on the day of the week or the season of the year. In our household that's just the way it was. My father would be up at 4:30; my mother, soon after that, and by the time I was up, the house would be bustling with activity, the smell of coffee, the aroma of my father's tobacco, and the cacophony of sounds emanating from pots, pans, dishes, mugs, and cutlery.

All through college, while I was away from home, no matter how late I hit the sack, I'd be up at 5:30. The question then is this: Was that a habit or was that the result of discipline?

It is a habit and not a discipline. But for many people waking up at 6:30 requires the discipline of a monk. It is not part of them to wake up at a certain time of day. One of my roommates in college (briefly) could not wake up till 10 minutes before his first class—which he went out of his way to schedule no earlier than 10 a.m. Don't get me wrong, he did well in life—this is not a story of waking up early and doing well because of it. He went on to build a successful startup after college and since then he has become a serial entrepreneur with four IPOs under his belt. He still wakes up at 10 a.m.

The point is about habits and discipline. Habits come naturally—and you should cherish habits if you've got the good ones. But discipline is the force that you use to alter the trajectory of those habits. Look at it this way. Think of the space shuttle that is on a trajectory. Its inertia is carrying it on a given trajectory—what is required to alter that trajectory or to bring it to a stop? Well, that's what those thrusters are for in the front of its nose. A little blast here, a little blast there, and you get minor course corrections that alter its trajectory. That's discipline.

Changing Trajectory

Discipline is the force that moves the inertia you have gained. So if you have taken on a habit of smoking—that sway the habit has on you is a trajectory that will move your life, and if you do nothing else, that trajectory will chart a course across your life. But to alter that habit requires that you apply minor course corrections to get you out of that trajectory.

With that overview in mind, let's look at the discipline of a Stoic and see the areas that it is applied, how it is applied, and to what end.

A Stoic's discipline is unforced. It is natural and this is unfamiliar to the rest of those of us who aspire to live the Stoic way. No Stoic feels discipline as something that is forced and painful, requiring effort, sacrifice, and suffering. It's like a child forced to do homework while his favorite cartoon plays for the one and only time on TV. And just like the kid who is forced to do something because of misplaced priorities, we feel the pain when required to do the right thing.

It is a matter of perspectives, isn't it? It's like the game show where the host knows what's behind the door, but the contestant doesn't and he is filled with worry and chaos as he tries to choose the right door. But for the host, the choice is obvious.

A parent and child have the same interactive relationship, the older knowing what is best, the younger knowing what is fun. The Stoic and the non-Stoic have the same relationship. The Stoic is loyal to the best course of action; the rest struggle with what feels good.

But there really isn't a choice, is there? The course of action is typically known and appreciated, but it is the cacophony of distractions that make the action untenable. We mistake this as wisdom in many cases when all it really is, is misplaced priorities and the lack of discipline to correct the course deviation.

So the question remains. What is a Stoic's discipline? As you may have started to uncover, the Stoic's discipline is about loyalty to doing the right thing. So what? Why is the right thing so important? Because the right thing is paid for or rewarded in the future. You can think of it as an annuity. You deposit something now and it pays off slowly over time. Discipline is about making the choice so that you maximize that slow payout in the future. You do what is necessary now so that all that unfolds over the course of time accrues as benefit. Doing the wrong thing now, no matter how pleasurable, yields a series of unfortunate catastrophes that snowball over time. Sometimes it even passes from one's own life and into the life of one's children.

Before we go any further, perhaps now is good a time as any to make one thing clear about the Stoic's worldview. There is no right and wrong when it comes to the Stoic's perspective—at least not in the sense that the rest see it.

No Right or Wrong

The Stoic's core tenet is that there is no good or bad, no right or wrong. But even without this binary set of choices, they are able to come out ahead in most scenarios. How is that even possible? Because it turns out that this universe is not built on right and wrong but on chaos and peace. There is a delicate balance of chaos and peace that pervades the fabric of everything that makes up this universe—everything that we can detect, and everything that we can't. This universe is a balance of chaos and silence. But do not make the mistake of thinking that one is energy and the other, a void. Both are forms of energy, and when in balance, they cancel each other out. But that balance is elusive and constantly oscillates from one state to the other.

It is like a pendulum moving from a point of dynamic imbalance to momentary equilibrium and then back again. This, in the view of a Stoic, is the metronome of the universe. Everything else big, small, and immeasurable, follows this pace. That includes all things tangible and all things intangible. From the balance of night and day, to the beat of the heart, to the vibrations of the atom, to the waxing and waning from inspiration to depression.

This allows the Stoic to see things differently, and it's not just a perspective. The way they see it encompasses most of all the perspectives, and they see it in an almost omnipotent way—I say "almost" because it would be impossible to see it all absolutely—there are perspectives that we are unable to perceive and experience without the necessary senses.

When you speak to a Stoic, and many have said this about men, including Marcus Aurelius, you may feel like the Stoic is able to see right through you and is not far from the truth. When you distill all things down to this chaos and peace framework, you start to understand the landscape of motivations each person has and the actions that flow from those motivations. When you are in that state, it is not hard to see why people do the things they do. It's like a parent who can see through the shenanigans of the child even before they think of doing something.

When you see discipline through this framework then it no longer looks like the baggage of effort that we think needs to be carried in order to get something done. Discipline then just becomes what it is—the conviction to do the right thing.

Stoics are composed and stoic—as the name implies, not because they are forcing themselves to be uncaring, but because they see a higher game at play, and the minor variances of feelings and emotions are just not perceptible to their senses, nor are they prioritized in their consciousness.

It is not just the way one looks at things, but the way one fosters his or her state of being. Think about the state of a child who wants to stay up past his bedtime and does not get his parents' approval. The parents know that the short-term benefit of going to bed late in no way outweighs the long-term benefit of rest and forming good habits for a young child. And so the tears of the child don't even come close to figuring into the responsible parent's decision. It is similar to how a Stoic sees most things.

Being in State

But what has all this got to do with discipline? The state you are in has everything to do with discipline. If you are not in the state to do something then you need a huge amount of effort to do it, and the outcome is not nearly as probable as it would be if you are in the right state. A Stoic's state is one that matches the task that he is about to undertake—no matter how devastating his surroundings or his circumstances.

Let me give you an example of how this plays out in life. Michael Schumacher is the world record holder for the most World Championship F1 titles. He has eight, by the way, and it is not an easy feat by any standard. From the first time I watched him win the championship the thing that occurred to me was his state of calm. I took it for granted that it was practiced. But that was not the case. In 2003, just before the race weekend, his mother was hospitalized in Italy and Schumacher visited her the day before the race. It was the last time he would see her. She passed just hours before his next race at Imola. For anyone, that would have been more than an acceptable reason to step out of the race. In fact, for a normal person that would have been advisable. The psychological stresses that occur during the race could tip a person who is already under emotional strain. But not only did he stick with it, he drove one of the most perfect races to win that circuit. He took each turn with precision; each straight with charge; and each nose-to-nose battle with grace. It was one of the most amazing races I have ever witnessed. He was in a state –the zone, as athletes call it.

When you are in this state, you do not need to force yourself to do the things that need to be done. You do not need the discipline to bend your hesitance into will.

You do not need to force the tasks necessary to accomplish the final goal. As such, when you are in this state, the future unfolds almost effortlessly.

Just like everything else, our decision-making process is also a habit. Each individual takes a specific path in coming to a decision and then coming to an action plan. There are two kinds of decisions, the first being the ones we plan on doing, and the second ones being the ones we actually execute. In many cases they are one and the same, but in a number of people what is planned is never what is executed. For a Stoic, what is executed is what was planned.

Think of the decision-making process as a path; it is just like the path you take when you drive to the store or the office. It is predictable and it is habitual. A person doesn't make bad decisions because he wants to face difficulty; a person makes bad decisions because he doesn't know any other path to take from where he stands to the point of the action.

While we look at discipline as the effort to push an action, a Stoic's discipline is about moving from one state to the next, depending on the task and goal at hand.

How does one make that happen?

If you are looking to understand Stoicism, there are a

few books you can turn to, the most important being *Meditations*, by Emperor Marcus Aurelius. Even that book was not something that Emperor Marcus chose to publish. It wasn't until much later that historians compiled his notes and placed them in book form. There are very few books that were written on this topic, fewer still that were translated well, and even fewer that have lasted till today.

What we do have are those who are innately Stoic who guide us with the principles of Stoicism. Then there are those of us who spend years reflecting, studying, testing and pushing the boundaries of what is considered life.

I encourage you to read as many interpretations as you can to get a better grasp of the many facets that encompass the Stoic's life.

Let's get back to the discipline of a Stoic.

To bring the Stoic's discipline into your life the first thing you need to do is embrace the ideals of a Stoic. We talked about this in the previous chapter—peace and truth.

Peace and truth are not what you used to think they were, but since you have had an introduction to them in the last chapter, it's time to take things deeper.

A Stoic is the embodiment of peace. Peace is not just the reward one gets for behaving and thinking in a certain way; peace is the state that reflects calm and understanding. Let's be clear: peace is also not about bending backwards and letting others trample over you. Peace is about knowing the secrets of nature and how things unfold.

Let's take, for instance, the concept of death. We all know that it exists, yet we are never prepared for it when it comes. Or are we?

Simple. Discipline, to most of us, is hard because we see it as the force required to change the trajectory of our decision-making process. The Stoic sees it as part and parcel of the outcome.

Chapter 6

Meditations of a Stoic

The meditations of a Stoic are not the same as the meditation methods and practices of Zen. They are certainly not the same as Hindu or other religious variations of meditations, and while all those forms serve their purpose, the point is that Stoic meditations are about conscious participation in the present.

Stoics are ardent believers and followers of the truth. When we mention truth in this world what we are talking about is the extension of our abilities to absorb the knowledge in the way knowledge should be, and without the emotional attachments humans typically place with it and with the biases we often taint it with.

Meditation is not about singular focus; it is about taking control of your field of gravity. It is unlike the meditation of doing nothing and merely breathing; it is about the power to do everything. A Stoic uses his breath to focus his mind to go beyond thinking.

Let me explain

The mind is divided into two areas. One is what we call

the conscious and the other is what we think of as the subconscious. To understand how Stoics see and live it, you need to be clear about the distinction between the two sides of your mind. The first is the side that you aware of and are conscious about. The thoughts that you cogitate, the memories that you ruminate over, the plans that you make, and even the arguments you have in your mind are the ones that are your conscious efforts. You know this very well; you deal with them on a daily basis.

Then there is the subconscious, and while there are many parts to it, we will look at them as one all-encompassing state of the brain. When you think of these two sides, it is easy to fall into the temptation to think of them as physical separations of physical sectors of the brain. But they are not physical. They are states of existence. Conscious levels are states that vary by degrees but for convenience are discussed as binary states of conscious and subconscious.

Comparing the States of Consciousness

The conscious side of you can be identified by your cognizance of its process. When you cogitate, think about life, reminisce with memories, work out a math problem, even talk with yourself as you debate a course of action, we refer to this as a conscious process.

An unconscious or subconscious process (which in psychology material is treated as two distinct issues) is treated as a process that is not apparent to your awareness. It happens in the background. It's much like keying in a calculator and a number popping out in response. We are unaware via any indication or awareness that anything is happening within the circuitry of the calculator. But there is a lot going on. The brain is similar in this regard.

The reason it makes no sense of us to be aware of what is going on in the circuitry of the calculator is because it is happening at such a fast rate that we cannot keep up with it, and so it is better if those rapid processes are left invisible.

The subconscious is the same way; it happens so rapidly that the conscious mind is not designed to deal with it. And that is purposely designed that way. Imagine what it would seem like if our subconscious was running the way it does and we were clued into the speed it was moving at—we would be extremely hyper and need to be sedated.

You can think about it this way: Imagine watching your favorite play on stage while all the background hands are in plain sight moving props around and getting ready for the next scene. It would completely distract from the actual play and would be unnecessary. Think of the play on the stage as the conscious process, while all the things that go on in the background are the subconscious.

But keep that analogy for as long as you can use it and not a minute longer. It will serve you well at the initial stages to think of the conscious and subconscious mind in this way.

The Stoic understands the difference between the two states of being—the conscious and the subconscious. The Stoic understands the importance of both and the appropriate use of both. Earlier on we mentioned in passing that the Stoic uses all of his mind in the moment while others don't seem to be able to do more than one thing at once. Let me reconcile that with this part of the book.

The being is divided between conscious and subconscious, but the subconscious is a group of so many different aspects. For instance, your heartbeat is subconscious, and so is the regulating of the heartbeat (to increase or decrease the beating rate). Your vasodilation is also controlled by the subconscious areas of the brain and an overwhelming quantum of the brain's resources are left to the area that is subconscious. Even the process of retrieving a memory is not something that you can consciously pinpoint. When you want to remember something, most of the time it appears, like a muse on stage, and then when done, quietly slips off the stage and you don't seem it anymore. But just because you do not see the muse exit stage-left, go around backstage, change costume, and reappear stage-right, doesn't mean it didn't happen.

Stoics understand exactly what they need to see and what they don't and that makes a difference towards how they solve or improve on the blessings that come their way. There are two sides of the coin and you can only see one side at a time, but it doesn't mean the other side does not exist. This is, in essence, the Stoic's secret.

As for the Stoic, not only does he see it; he is clearly in control of both. The reason he is able to do that is because he understands the subconscious mind. Being aware of it is the first half of the game. Controlling it is the second, and that's where meditation comes into play.

Meditation

Meditation, for the Stoic, is not in any way similar to the way others practice it. It is not for the sake of relaxing, nor is it to calm the day, or even to just reflect. It is all that but also a lot more. If you are already into meditation then you will need to up your game by at least one order of magnitude.

It may sound hyperbolic, but it's not. The Stoic's

strength comes from efficient use of his entire being, putting aside what is meant to be in the moment and calculating and analyzing everything else. Here is a good test. If you were to think of a simple sum, two plus two, you could work out the answer without actually thinking of it. If I raise the ante and ask you to think about 9 x 8, you could probably pull it off and answer 72. But what if I asked you to multiply 18 x 19? You'd probably have to work it out and you would do it consciously. You would go through the steps and after about four and five steps you would arrive at the answer.

The part of you going through the steps is the conscious side of you. But what if I told you that it is entirely possible to not have to consciously work at the steps but allow the much faster subconscious side of you do that? Chances are you would believe me because you have seen all the memory tricks online that show you how to do it. But I assure you it is not a trick. Stoics don't perform ticks.

The Stoics are masters of separating mental cogitations and functions based on the most efficient utilization of resources. After all, you wouldn't use a tractor to race NASCAR, and you wouldn't use a Bugatti to plow the field, would you? The same goes towards the use of the brain.

The Stoic is aware of separating the tools of his mind to carry the appropriate weight. He keeps his present moment intact with the light lifting and passes the heavy loads to his much faster, more effective subconscious mind.

There are a few problems when one does that. The first is that the conscious mind still tries to wrestle with the heavy lifting and the second is that when the answer is ready from the subconscious, a regular person is not able to recognize the solution.

How does the Stoic know the right answer? It comes from intense discipline in being able to move instructions to the subconscious, strict discipline in not overworking the conscious by worrying, and finally, knowing when the answer is being served up by the subconscious.

And so the follow-up question is, how does one get that discipline and know how to communicate with the subconscious? That is the purpose of meditation.

The Stoic's meditation is about the discipline of silence. It is different from reflection, and very different from the mindfulness that you hear about so often these days. You need all three to be able to perform as a Stoic does and that is the advanced step of the Stoic. Let's start with a Stoic's reflection exercise and see what it means to reflect on one's day, one's actions, or even one's past.

Unlike other scenarios where we look at mindfulness first then build up to reflection and then build up to the climax of meditation, the Stoic's meditation starts at the ability to meditate. Because, for the Stoic, meditation is the central part of being able to perform during the day. It is the core of his reflection and it is the flavor of his mindfulness.

You can do it both ways, but his is the way of the Stoic.

Remember, the purpose of meditation is twofold. The first is to train the subconscious to do the heavy lifting and the second is to train the conscious to be silent and wait to receive guidance from the subconscious.

When you divide the responsibility, you will find that no problem is too small and no opponent, especially one who doesn't meditate, that can't be overcome. □

Conclusion

I take significant umbrage with much of the available paraphernalia that tries to list steps to becoming a Stoic. It can't be done that way. Every Stoic knows that the path to Stoicism is not one that is taken by rigid steps and tasks. Even if you can start off this way, to give you an idea of what it is, you cannot possibly expect to embrace Stoicism from those kinds of cookbook-like pamphlets.

Stoicism is within you, and that is why Stoicism is the result of deep reflection and even deeper introspection. To do that you have to do as René Descartes advises and read concepts and observations of others and deeply compare them to what you know to be true from your own experiences, then slowly replace and alter the knowledge set that you have with the new.

You can also use the shoebox method I taught my kids, but instead of doing it with fact-based information, you can use it to ask question about the things you observe. In practice, it would like something like this:

If the fact-based questions look like this: "What is the moon made of?" then the observation-based questions will look like this: "Why do we fear things we don't know?"

Can you appreciate the subtle difference?

The path to Stoicism is not just about answering the questions. If that was the case, any fool with a good Internet connection could be considered a Stoic or could be deemed enlightened. It's not just about finding answers; it is about knowing what to ask. That only comes from reflection.

The Bible says something that has struck me for a long time. "Ask and ye shall receive." In my youth, I never understood the full power of that phrase and always took it to mean that I could ask for a bike and get it, ask for a box of chocolates and get it, and so on. But to my little heart's dismay, none of what I asked for came to fruition. The bicycle I wanted remained in the store until some other kid bought it. The box of chocolates was always turned down and was completely shot after the dentist went on a tirade about the detriment of candy. You get the point.

But as I grew up, I realized that that advice of ask and receive was not akin to a genie in a bottle, but more about how the universe transmits information. I realized that the path to asking the right question is made up of starting with the first question—any question—the second box. When I made it a habit to ask questions, it started to pop up everywhere. And the more I asked, the more I filled up the second box, the more answers came to me via observation and so I managed to fill that third box.

That's what Stoicism is. The rest of it, the meditation, the reflection, the fasting, the appearance is all just secondary and in support of that ability to ask, observe, hypothesize, and ask some more. Rinse and repeat.

We are all Stoics at birth—at least we have what it takes to be one. It is what comes after that which distracts us and turns our Stoic nature on its head. Then, if we are lucky, we find the term Stoic somewhere, are intrigued by its nature, and start asking questions. Then we stumble across literature and we do what we can to find our way back to it.

Embracing Stoicism is really a coming home.

Spoiler alert. You can choose to keep reading the last paragraph, or you can go build your life as a Stoic then come back in a year and read this part to see if you have come to the same conclusion.

There is only knowledge. That is the only thing that is real. That means that only the intangible is real and all else is built on that. Flesh, bones, buildings, and stones are all built on top of the fundamental vibrations of energy, and that energy is the essence that we can look at as knowledge.

To be clear, I don't mean knowledge as knowing the date when something happened or the height of the highest mountain—I do not mean data. I mean the knowledge of the universe. Some people call it the soul of the universe. In the end, only knowledge subsists. It is the only thing that can exist in the vacuum of time. It is the only thing that can be passed on from one lifetime to the next, one universe to the next, and it is all that matters to the Stoic. Once you get that secret, then all else becomes minuscule by comparison.

Stoicism knows that peace and truth are the attributes of this knowledge. When you embrace peace and truth you approach the knowledge that is sought. When you embrace that knowledge then the peace and truth you seek are fulfilled. Go after the knowledge and jettison all else. It is a distraction from the highest truth and a hurdle to ultimate peace.

Thank You!

Before you go, I would like to thank you for purchasing a copy of my book. Out of the dozens of books you could have picked over mine, you decided to go with this one and for that I am very grateful.

I hope you enjoyed reading it as much as I have enjoyed writing it! I hope you found it very informative.

I would like to ask you for a small favor. <u>Could you please take a moment to leave a review for this book on Amazon?</u>

Your feedback will help me continue to write more books and release new content in the future!

More Books by Garry

- Stoicism: Understanding Stoicism in Context of the Modern World
- Stoicism: A Stoic's Journey: A Practical Guide to Practicing Stoicism
- Affirmations: Powerful Affirmations to Empower the Subconscious Mind to Achieve Anything
- Manifesting: How to Use the Law of Attraction to Manifest Your Dreams

Printed in Great Britain
by Amazon